AF439841

Table of Contents

Introduction

Whether you grow food on a spacious homestead or are digging into your first urban garden, ditching the plant-by-rows approach and instead adopting intensive gardening techniques can help you grow a more productive garden that's also more efficient to manage. These methods will open up a new world when it comes to small-space gardening, which can be so much more than just a few lone pots on a balcony. If you do it right, you can grow more food in less space and put an impressive dent in your household's fresh-food needs.

Comparing 2 Popular Intensive Gardening Methods

Two gardening authors and their systems of intensive vegetable gardening have been highly influential in North America for more than 30 years. Mel Bartholomew's book on "square-foot" gardening was first published in 1981, while John Jeavons' first book on "biointensive" gardening came out in 1974. Since these books hit the shelves, millions of gardeners have experimented with and embraced the gardening techniques advocated within.

Bartholomew's aim with square-foot gardening is a simple, foolproof system that anyone can master (no companion planting, no crop rotation and no soil preparation). He prescribes raised beds of only 6 inches deep for most crops, filled with an artificial mix of peat moss, vermiculite and compost. While this method is reliant on assembling purchased components, it can work well in urban spaces, especially where soil contamination is a concern, where digging into the ground isn't an option, or where people are especially picky about how a garden looks (perhaps because of ordinances for front lawns).

Jeavons' biointensive gardening system is based on developing fertile soil in permanent garden beds that you initially dig to a depth of 2 feet. His primary goal is to grow food sustainably, using as few inputs from outside of the system as possible. He provides detailed instructions on crop planning, making compost, companion planting, crop rotation, growing crops that serve a dual purpose as food and compost-heap fodder, and more.

4 Principles of Intensive Gardening

Despite such differing approaches, both sets of techniques deliver high-yielding food gardens thanks to four common features, all of which I recommend.

1. Permanent garden beds. Establishing permanent beds enables you to concentrate your efforts only on where plants grow, without wasting compost or irrigation water on unplanted areas. It also makes soil compaction a nonissue, because you walk on permanent pathways and never on your growing areas. Setting up permanent beds and paths is such a popular layout here in the Pacific Northwest that I haven't seen a garden arranged in rows for years.

2. Reliance on compost. Both systems rely on the tried-and-true groundwork of all organic gardening: heavy doses of compost to supply balanced, slow-release nutrients needed to grow healthy crops. The organic matter in compost also increases soil's water-holding capacity and improves its texture.

3. High-density mixed planting. A key to the high productivity of both systems is that they take advantage of the entire surface of each bed to grow plants rather than leaving spaces between rows. This results in even more yield without adding more garden space. For novice gardeners, Bartholomew's method of marking off beds in 1-foot squares may be particularly helpful as a way to visualize how densely one can plant. Interspersing crops with different root depths, plant heights and growth rates also means you can grow more in a given space.

4. Prompt succession planting. Staggered planting and, thus, staggered harvests are more efficient for the gardener and maximize the growing season. Quickly

replanting any gaps left after harvesting a particular crop lets you use every area of the garden throughout the year.

Customize Your Intensive Gardening System

With fertile soil and dense planting, any garden can be highly productive — but as these two intensive-gardening approaches show, you can achieve this productivity via different means. I'm on Bartholomew's side in favoring simple, low-maintenance methods (after all, the energy of the gardener is a valuable resource, too), but gardeners can learn much from Jeavons about sustainable practices. Reducing the use of nonrenewable resources — whether it's fossil fuels burned in transporting supplies, irrigation water from deep aquifers or even peat moss — is an important consideration and one that's on many gardeners' minds. Square-foot gardening calls for purchasing a large amount of peat moss, which isn't a renewable material. Coconut coir is a more sustainable option.

With time and experience, and based on the region and circumstances, every gardener tailors his or her system to what works best. I've talked with hundreds of gardeners over the past few decades to glean some of the commonalities between successful gardening systems, and the resulting recommendations that follow here will help you grow a high-yield but low-maintenance, sustainable garden.

Adapt to local conditions. Soil, climate, weather, water availability, composting materials, pests and diseases vary depending on where you live, so learn from local experts and look for information written for your region. The space you have available and the ease with which you can transport materials will also influence your gardening decisions. If you have a tiny urban garden, you aren't likely to be able to grow a considerable amount of grain crops for supplying carbonaceous compostable materials, as Jeavons suggests doing. Creating nutrients and organic matter by making compost out of other ingredients, such as fall leaves and newspapers mixed with food scraps, may make more sense. For a large garden with more space, however, growing compostable or "green manure" crops may be the most practical way to build the organic matter in your soil.

Go permanent. The effectiveness of using permanent garden beds is undisputed. Whether permanent beds should be raised, however, depends on the site and on personal preference. Raised beds — constructed with sides to allow the soil to be built up higher than the natural soil level — allow for good drainage on low-lying land and warm up quickly in spring. Older and less mobile folks could benefit from raised beds because they're higher up and easier to work in. Gardens on well-drained soil, however, may fare better and need less water if the beds are not raised — and, of course, you won't have the job and expense of building sides for your beds.

Use soil (if you have it). A con of Bartholomew's system is that it relies so heavily on buying the ingredients to make your growing medium. This is expensive and means you aren't using and improving the soil already on your property. Despite Bartholomew's concern that improving soil takes too long, I've found that adding organic amendments, including balanced organic fertilizers if needed, can turn any soil into decent garden soil in its first few seasons. Generous applications of compost increase the nutrient- and water-holding capacity of sandy soils and improve the structure of clay soils. Regarding water conservation, plants growing in the ground usually need less irrigation than plants in containers or raised beds do, because soil-bound plants benefit from capillary flow of water from the subsoil. This upward movement of water can come from a depth of 2 to 8 feet, depending on the type of soil. Deep-rooted plants will also survive cold snaps and heat waves better than plants in containers and raised beds because their roots are subjected to less-extreme temperature swings. Of course, if your best sunny spot is a paved parking lot, by all means, build raised beds (the deeper, the better).

Be cheap. The first time I read Bartholomew's book, I was struck by how expensive following his system to the letter would be, from the cost of building beds to buying and hauling a large volume of bulky materials for the growing medium — which he calls "Mel's mix." To me, the beauty of gardening is that it transforms waste material into tasty, nourishing food at a considerably lower cost than buying it. Compost can be virtually free if made from waste materials, such as grass clippings, leaves, manure, spoiled hay, and any waste from your garden, the grocery store or the food industry. Perhaps the ultimate in cheap fertilizer is "pee-cycling," which merits wider acceptance for its effectiveness.

Don't work too hard. When I initially encountered Jeavons' book in the 1970s, I set out to follow his technique for double-digging my garden. I quickly discovered, despite Jeavons' cheery instructions, that this was a daunting amount of work. When you finish shifting the soil, you will have moved all of the soil in the bed sideways by 1 or 2 feet and down to a depth of 2 feet. After digging one bed, I decided to skip the rest and live with the consequences — except none seemed to crop up. I saw no difference between the double-dug bed and the rest of the garden throughout that summer or in later years. Similarly, a 1998 study by Ohio State

University found no significant yield difference between beans and beets grown in beds that had been cultivated only on the surface and beds that had been double-dug.

Over many years of intensive gardening, I have learned (as have many gardeners before me) that layering on mulches saves a lot of labor, and that minimal cultivation of beds works just fine. Research has provided sound reasons why minimizing soil disturbance is a good idea: Reduced-tillage systems result in higher populations of beneficial fungi that move nutrients and water through the soil column. Also, soils that receive less disruption have more beneficial nematodes, earthworms, soil mites and other microorganisms wriggling and crawling about. Neither Bartholomew's artificial planting medium nor Jeavons' repeated double-digging takes full advantage of such hardworking critters.

Because earthworms, plant roots and soil insects are so good at aerating soil, I'm happy to leave it to them. Without turning over the soil, I lightly fork compost and other amendments into the top couple of inches once a year, which takes me about 15 minutes for an 8-by-4-

foot bed. For the rest of the season, I plant without cultivating, allowing easy interplanting by slipping in new plants between maturing crops. I often leave crop residues on the soil as a mulch and plant right through it. Creating minimal disturbance has led to a bountiful garden with less work on my part. This can, however, require a slight shift from the "clean soil" garden aesthetic some value.

Weeding is, for most, a dreaded task, but it can be almost eliminated by smart planting. Intensive planting suppresses weeds, as the leaves of nearby plants quickly fill in and shade the soil. Using mulch to keep the soil covered is effective at smothering germinating weed seeds. I leave mulch on the soil for as much of the garden season as possible (weeds grow all winter in my Northwest climate), but I pull it back in spring to allow the soil to dry out and warm up. You can control weeds in pathways by laying down cardboard, newspaper or other light-excluding materials, or sow the pathways to grass or clover and mow (or scythe) them every now and then. Put the clippings back on the garden beds as a nitrogen-rich mulch.

Making compost can be as simple as putting everything in a bin, waiting for a season to pass, and then spreading the most digested material on the garden and returning undigested material to the bin. Or, don't make compost at all: Just leave organic material on the soil to decompose. Any plant material, including crop residues and pulled weeds, will impart organic matter as soil organisms break it down. Roots are another source of organic matter, so instead of pulling plants when clearing a bed, I cut them at the soil line and leave the roots to decompose.

Keep it simple. My eyes glaze over when I see equations and complicated charts in a gardening book, and Bartholomew's and Jeavons' books aren't short on either. While I generally vote for skipping overcomplicated and prescriptive planting advice, I do think keeping basic gardening records is useful. They don't need to be elaborate, but recording when and what you plant, harvest dates, and notes on pest problems is a good idea so you have this information and can make well-informed adjustments when you plan next year's garden.

Ignore the bewildering number of gardening rules and myths floating around the Internet and other sources. For example, companion-planting charts of the "tomatoes love basil" variety are largely myth, though the value of planting to cycle nutrients to different crop families and attract beneficial insects is well-established. In my experience, you can safely disregard most crop-rotation systems, because relatively few crops in a diverse food garden are likely to suffer from soilborne diseases or pests. After you know what problems occur in your region, you know which crops to rotate. Where I live, for example, the high risk of root disease in the onion family and for potatoes makes four-year crop rotations smart for these, but I don't worry about allowing long rotations for other vegetables.

Relax and smile. Gardens should be individualistic and fun. They can be as tidy or as wild as you like, take little effort to maintain, and still produce an astonishing amount of food from a small area. If digging beds, turning compost or setting up growing boxes works for you, carry on — just don't think any of it is a strict requirement for a bountiful garden. Personally, I figure the less time and effort it takes to grow food, the more time there is to enjoy it!

10 Tenets of Square-Foot Gardening

1. Cultivate in small, raised garden boxes that are at least 6 inches deep, separated into a 1-by-1-foot grid pattern (often 16 squares per box).

2. Fill boxes with a growing medium made of one-third peat moss, one-third vermiculite and one-third blended compost.

3. Intensively plant a prescribed number of each crop you choose to grow into each grid space, depending on plant size. (See Bartholomew's book for the prescribed numbers. For example, plant one broccoli per square and plant 16 carrots per square.)

4. Sow only the number of seeds needed in each square to avoid wasting seed.

5. Add no fertilizer; rely on the compost in the growing medium for nutrients.

6. Practice low-maintenance gardening, with no digging, tilling, soil prep, soil testing or cultivating.

7. Achieve staggered harvests with succession planting.

8. Capitalize on vertical space by growing vining crops on supports.

9. Leave wide aisles (at least 3 feet wide) between your growing boxes to easily work in your beds and maneuver between them.

10. Employ tools minimally — you should only need a trowel for transplanting, a pencil for poking holes and lifting seedlings out of pots, and scissors for harvesting.

10 Tenets of Biointensive Gardening

1. Loosen soil in raised-bed planting sites by "double-digging" to a depth of 2 feet.

2. Space crops tightly in a hexagonal planting pattern.

3. Apply no chemicals.

4. Compost on-site and use compost to amend and build your soil.

5. Use synergistic planting (also called "companion planting") so that plants grown together enhance each other.

6. Plant dual-purpose, carbon-efficient crops — such as grains — in about 60 percent of the growing area. (Such crops provide a significant amount of dietary calories as well as a significant amount of carbonaceous material for composting.)

7. Grow calorie-efficient root crops, such as potatoes, in about 30 percent of the growing area.

8. Sow open-pollinated seeds to preserve genetic diversity.

9. Create a "closed," interrelated growing system in which enough organic matter is produced by your "mini-farm" to sustain the soil within the system.

10. Produce food in a way that, compared with conventional farming, greatly reduces the use of resources, and places a focus on diversity, soil building and achieving high yields.

Intensive Planting In The Vegetable Garden

Intensive vegetable gardening is the name given to a way of using garden space and soil nutrients to produce high yields of flavorful crops.

The intensive planting method of vegetable gardening is perhaps the most efficient and effective of all growing methods. It is both resource-conserving and sustainable.

The origins of this method can be traced back 4,000 years to ancient China. Two thousand years ago similar approaches were in use in Latin America, Europe, and parts of Asia. Just more than 100 years ago, market vegetable gardeners around Paris began using this method to supply fresh vegetables to urban shoppers; intensive planting produced enough food for a large population on relatively scarce land.

Modern vegetable gardeners call intensive garden by many names: the Chinese way to garden, French intensive gardening, biodynamic gardening, and more recently Postage Stamp and Square Foot gardening.

Backyard gardeners can easily employ intensive gardening methods to increase both the variety and yield of crops they grow.

Here are the principles and methods of intensive vegetable gardening:

Soil improvement: The soil is well-prepared before planting. The site for planting is cleared of all weeds and debris then 3 to 4 inches of organic matter is spread over the site and dug or tilled into the soil. Aged compost, well-rotted manure, grass clippings, chopped leaves, or combinations of these are the most nutrient-rich amendments for vegetable growing. It is best to add amendments to the soil a month or more before planting; this allows nutrients to disperse throughout the soil. Later a mulch of compost is spread across the bed to prevent rain and wind from washing or blowing away the soil. The soil can be pre-warmed with plastic mulch—black or clear plastic sheeting spread—before sowing or transplanting crops.

Narrow beds also called wide rows: Intensive planting means spacing crops closely. Plants are arranged two three or more plants or rows across a single bed—called a narrow bed or wide row. Seeds are sown or transplants are set in the garden so that their leaves grow to just touch at maturity; nearly every inch of growing space in a bed is used for growing. Permanent pathways run between planting beds. The number of plants in a narrow bed or wide row varies according to how far the gardener can reach. Once a bed or wide row is planted, the gardener never steps onto the growing soil; she simply reaches arm's length into the bed to plant, tend, and harvest each crop. Narrow beds and wide rows make it easier to sustain soil improvement. Plant nutrients and water are never wasted on pathways or unplanted space between crops.

Raised beds: Raised beds are planting beds dedicated to growing crops season after season. A raised bed can be any shape but most commonly is rectangular or square. A simple raised bed can be created by simply hoeing up soil to make a bed that is higher than the surrounding soil. Spread ground cover bark, compost, or lay stepping stones into the pathways between beds. Raised beds are the home for narrow beds or wide rows. A raised bed should not be wider than the gardener's reach to the center of the bed from either side—3 to 5 feet is common. Raised beds should not be any longer than the distance the gardener wants to walk to get to the other side; don't be tempted to cut across your raised beds. A permanent raised bed can be created by bordering the bed a frame of lumber, cement blocks, or stones.

Succession planting: Following one crop with another crop is called succession planting. Succession planting allows you to increase your harvest without making your garden larger. For example follow a crop of spring lettuce with summer growing tomatoes, peppers, or eggplants. Then late in the summer, follow the summer-growing crops with cool-season crops such as lettuce or spinach. Succession planting takes a bit of planning; you will need to know how many days to maturity each crop takes and how many days you have in your growing season—that is the number of days from the last frost in spring to the first frost in fall.

Companion planting: The term companion planting can mean different things to different gardeners. Companion planting can include: (1) Planting different kinds of crops together in a garden bed to make the best use of garden space and each crop's growing habit to increase the overall yield. This type of companion planting is called inter-cropping, for example, planting a low growing crop that requires shade between two taller growing crops. (2) Planting specific flowering plants near a vegetable garden to attract beneficial and pollinating insects, and also planting plants that will attract a particular pest; that, in turn, protects a desired crop from damage. This type of companion planting is called trap-cropping. (3) Planting specific crops alongside one another to improve the flavor of one of the crops. This type of companion planting is based on folk tradition and has not been scientifically proven. For example, old-time garden tradition says planting dill next to cabbage will improve the flavor of the cabbage.

Crop rotation: Crop rotation means planting crops in an order that maintains or enhances soil fertility. Some crops are heavy feeders—meaning they use lots of nutrients in the soil; other crops are light feeders; and some crops are soil builders; they actually give nutrients back to the soil. Heavy feeders include tomatoes, broccoli, cabbage, corn, eggplants, beets, lettuce, and other leafy crops. Heavy feeders are planted after light feeders; light feeders include garlic, onions, peppers, potatoes, radishes, rutabagas, sweet potatoes, Swiss chard, and turnips. Soil builders include peas, beans, and cover crops like clover. Soil builders are planted after light feeders.

You can implement an intensive gardening program in your vegetable garden by introducing each of these elements into your garden—in just the order presented here.

Intensive Gardening Makes Small Spaces Work Double Time

For most of us, the agrarian ideal—a traditional vegetable garden, with evenly spaced single rows gently curving over a large, rectangular plot—is neither possible nor practical. Thankfully, many far more productive and equally tested planting methods are accessible and achievable for today's new crop of vegetable gardeners. Often described as intensive gardening methods, these practices help you produce more in less space.

Choose High-yield Crops

Planting crops that have a high yield per square foot makes better use of limited space. Tomatoes, peppers, onions, eggplant, beans, cucumbers and summer squash offer a lot of produce throughout the season from just a few plants. Also high-yielding, lettuce and greens are described as "cut-and-come-again" crops, meaning that you can cut the outer leaves continually through the growing season and the plant will continue to produce more leaves from the center. On the other hand, long vining crops such as melons, pumpkins and winter squash (such as butternut and acorn) require a lot of space for a relatively small harvest. One-harvest crops like cabbage and broccoli are also less efficient (though you can get second-harvest side-shoots from broccoli).

Plant Wide Rows

When you think about it more closely, the single-row method is really kind of a waste of space. The gaps between rows aren't ripe for much beyond soil compaction (your feet are the culprits) and erosion. Instead, intensive gardeners will plant rows with two or three plants side-by-side, creating one wide double or triple row. This reduces the overall number of rows and the wasted space between them. Use the wide row method for all crops except vining plants like cucumbers and melons. It's an especially lovely and useful practice for lettuce and greens like kale and chard.

Grow in Raised Beds

If you have limited space, poor soil or a bad back, raised beds are a great option. You can design a raised bed to be any shape or size, and make it out of almost any material, such as wood, rock, metal or even straw bales. The real advantage of raised beds lies in the middle, where you add loose, fluffy, deep soil, ideal for growing vegetables. Because the soil in raised beds is ideal, you can space plants more closely together than you can in native soil. I am constantly amazed at how much I can grow in one 4- x 8-foot raised bed.

Try Vertical Gardening

When you run out of space on the ground, grow up instead. Vining plants such as cucumbers, beans, peas, squash and tomatoes grow easily on trellises or fences, which can be made of anything from wood to bamboo to string. I've found that metal cattle panels (or hog panels, found at farm supply stores) make extra-sturdy trellises. Train the plant onto the trellis and secure it with twine. Some heavier fruits like melons will need extra support (usually a sling made from stretchy material such as old pantyhose) if grown vertically.

Plant Crops Together

A planting method called interplanting or intercropping helps you use space more efficiently. One idea is to plant fast-growing vegetables among slower-growing ones, such as radishes (faster) among carrots (slower), so that you harvest the fast crop before it begins to crowd the slow one. You also can plant low-growing crops that can take a little shade—such as lettuce, greens and cool-season herbs like parsley and chives—under tall crops like tomatoes and peppers, where the lower level will catch the rays that the taller plants let filter through.

Extend the Season

I'm always amazed at gardeners who pack it up at the end of August and think the gardening season is over until the following May or June. Spring and fall are arguably the best times to garden! By planting in all seasons, you get more annual harvest out of your space, which is the ultimate goal of intensive gardening. Having a plan for succession planting also helps extend the season and increase overall yields. For example, I plant peas in late winter for spring harvest, and then pull them up as the weather gets warm and they begin to wither. I replace them with peppers, which I'm prepared to cover in the case of a late frost. In mid to late summer, when I've had my fill of chilies, I take up the peppers and plant greens for fall and winter harvest.

Intensive Gardening in Containers

Containers are the ultimate solution for gardeners with limited space. While containers themselves aren't really an intensive technique, you can employ intensive practices such as extending the season, vertical gardening and choosing high-yield crops and interplanting in your container garden. Some specialized containers, such as strawberry jars, also offer a kind of intensive planting because they allow you to grow from the top and the sides. Also look for compact new varieties of vegetable plants, such as cherry tomatoes, that were developed especially to suit small containers and even hanging baskets.

Intensive Gardening Method

For some people, a small-sized garden is preferable to a larger one. Smaller gardens require less labor and expense than larger gardens. Decreasing garden size provides more yard space for other activities. The gardener can concentrate soil improvement efforts in a smaller area, and, with careful management, small gardens can produce sufficient vegetables for fresh eating during the growing season, and perhaps extra produce for preserving.

For some gardeners a small garden is not practical. If you are interested in preserving, a smaller garden may not provide enough produce for winter use.

"Intensive" gardeners must pay close attention to scheduling plantings to ensure that no part of a smaller garden is left unoccupied. Some growing seasons can complicate trying to stagger plantings.

Smaller gardens also require careful management. Growing plants closer together demands particular attention to pest control, fertilization and training of plants. To grow all the vegetables you want, you may have to use transplants instead of direct seeding, which will increase your costs.

To manage smaller gardens successfully, gardeners must use different growing methods. These can include bed planting, vertical growing, inter-planting, and succession planting. Growing vegetables in containers is another type of intensive gardening and is described in Container Gardening.

Raised Beds

Raised beds are growing areas whose surface is "raised" above the surrounding area. Raised beds can be temporary or permanent. Once established, the garden traffic is confined to paths, which reduces soil compaction. Soil improvement efforts are focused on the beds alone, not in the paths. Raised beds warm faster and dry earlier in the spring, allowing earlier spring planting.

Disadvantages of Raised Beds

Raised beds are not the answer for all gardeners lacking space. The initial labor and cost to establish the beds may be high. Once established, especially with permanent "sides," it may be difficult to use a standard size plow or tiller for cultivation. The tendency of the soil in raised beds to dry faster may increase the need for irrigation later in the season. Also, not all types of vegetables grow well in bed culture.

One of the better things I did when I lived in the desert was put a drip hose in the beds of vegetables that needed the most water. That was a boon! And to think I could have saved myself all that trouble by NOT using raised beds in the first place! ARGH.

Types and Sizes of Raised Beds

Raised beds can be free-standing or built with more permanent sides to help hold the soil in place. You can first outline your freestanding beds by marking out a tilled area where you intend to make your beds. No need to till the path ways.

Make beds any convenient length, but not wider than four or five feet across for easy reaching from either side. (I guess it really just depends on how long your arms are!)

Once marked, you can use a hoe or rake to move soil from paths up into beds. Make freestanding beds no higher than eight inches or they will dry too quickly or be washed easily by rains. Finish by smoothing the top of the bed with a rake. At least if you like things neat and pretty like I do!

The beds will settle some through the growing season of course. To prevent excessive drying and washing of soil, mulch (mulch, MULCH!!) the sides of the beds with an organic mulch like straw, leaves or grass clippings.

Anything you can throw in a compost pile, you can use for mulch.

Permanent raised beds have supported sides. A variety of material including wood or concrete blocks can be used for the sides. Redwood or western red cedar of at least two-inch thickness are long-lasting, or you may use pressure-treated wood. DON'T make the same mistake I did! I got a number of railroad ties for free. The creosote they use to soak those things is really toxic. And it takes forEVER to stop leaching out into your soil!

You can make permanent raised beds for disabled gardeners, just raise them somewhat higher for easy reaching. The gardener can sit on the edge of the bed to work. You can even design wheelchair access growing beds to be three feet high and no more than two feet wide.

Once the sides are installed, fill beds with garden soil which has been amended with peat, shredded leaves, compost or other organic materials. If you get the soil from an unknown source I would strongly urge you to have it tested first. I once bought four ton of top soil and it took me two growing seasons to get it balanced in a way that would allow ANYTHING to grow in it! Live and Learn!

Since these beds will be in place a number of years, building up and loosening it's soil when first establishing the beds is important. Properly amended raised beds will have soil loose and friable enough to be turned easily with a shovel. Old mulch, compost or other organic material can be turned under each year which will further enrich the soil.

You also can organize your garden into beds, but not actually raise them. This is a good option for gardeners with sandy soil that would dry too quickly if formed in raised beds. Beds are a more efficient way to organize the garden than rows, especially for small-sized vegetables. By establishing permanent paths and beds (even if they're NOT raised) you still will avoid compacting the soil in growing areas.

Most crops are adaptable to growing in beds, but small-sized vegetables like lettuce, greens, dwarf or bush varieties and cabbage perform the best. Root crops like beets and carrots also will thrive in the looser soils of beds.

Whether raised or not, the advantage of beds is that vegetable plants can be grown more closely together. Space plants by thinning or transplanting so they are evenly spaced in the beds. The spacing should be whatever the seed packet recommends for spacing between plants. For example, if the seed packet says to thin lettuce so plants stand six inches apart in rows two feet apart, ignore the row spacing, and thin all lettuce plants to stand six inches apart. Root crops like carrots and beets still can be sown in rows, but plant two or three rows the length of the growing bed.

Plants like lettuce and radishes can be sown by lightly sprinkling seed over the bed and gradually thinning young plants to their recommended final spacing.

Trellis and Vertical Growing

Lots of gardeners use vertical growing to save space in the garden. Caging tomatoes and trellising peas are two familiar examples. Besides saving space, vegetables grown this way are easier to pick and may have less rot because the fruit does not contact the soil. Improved air circulation can even further reduce diseases. Growing plants vertically can mean higher yields per base area. Additionally, vegetable plants can be trained on trellises to provide welcome summer shade to smaller cooler seasonal things like lettuce, spinach, or beets; or privacy screens, as well as to produce food for the table.

Trellising does have some disadvantages, however. Climbing supports must be sturdy, especially in windy sites. Building and installing trellises can involve time and expense. If plants are not naturally twining, they will have to be trained or secured to trellises, and heavy fruit will require additional support.Transpiration is higher in plants growing upright, so they may require extra water. Flowers will be more exposed to the wind, which may discourage pollinators like bees, and can cause flower abortion.

Types and Installation

The type of vegetable determines what kind of trellis used. A wide variety of trellising materials is available. A good rule is to install the sturdiest trellis you can afford. There is simply NO describing the feeling of going outside after a high wind only to find your prize melons pushed over backward on the ground and the vine snapped in two at the base!!

If the trellis is part of your landscaping it should be aesthetically pleasing, too.

Posts or supports for trellises can be made from metal, wood or plastic like PVC pipe. Metal posts will last longer and are easier to install than wooden ones. Wooden posts should be treated with a preservative or they may last only one season.

The BEST thing in the world I have found are cattle panels. They are about four to five feet high and I connect them with steel posts. Just wire them on and VIOLA! They are cheap and they aren't hard to move around either!

Posts can be used to support plastic or string mesh, or chicken wire. (Did I just say chicken wire? No, you did NOT hear me say that! I swore I would never use than evil stuff again... I'd use plain string first... that stuff is awful! It's for CHICKENS... period.

Plastic and string meshes can be disposed of, plants and all, at clean-up time. Removing dead plants from chicken wire fencing is frustrating and futile.

Longer poles made of bamboo can be arranged in teepees to support climbing vegetables like pole beans.

You can make a vertical frame of electrical conduit fastened with slip fittings, or 1/2 inch water pipe with threaded elbow couplings (detail). Attach strings to support the plants. You can arrange vertical frames in a number of ways. Run them as a straight fence (upper left), in zigzag pattern (upper right), with space between the frames (lower left), or as an arbor (lower right).

All trellises or climbing supports should be installed while plants still are small to avoid disturbing the roots of course! Orient trellises to run in an east-west direction, and locate them on the north side of the garden to avoid shading other plants. (unless of course that's your intention!)

You can use slings to support fruit as it develops.

Melons and squashes do not naturally twine and will have to be trained initially by weaving stem ends through mesh openings. Developing fruit can be supported with slings made from used stockings or rags. Insect protection is an extra benefit of using slings, especially if the entire fruit is wrapped.

Most gardeners practice a simple succession planting in row gardens by following a lettuce planting in spring with a late crop of, say, beans, or by staggering plantings of beans or sweet corn to ensure a steady harvest. Staggered plantings also work well with lettuce, radishes and other fast-yielding crops.

I've even been known to plant lettuce under my corn so it has plenty of shade. Carrots grow especially well this way. Be warned! Succession planting demands careful attention to days-to-maturity for each vegetable you plant, and attention to soil fertility to keep the intensively planted vegetables growing well.

Schedule plantings so no area of the garden remains empty for long. Remember that later planted succession crops mature faster than earlier planted ones because growing conditions, especially temperature and light intensity, usually are more favorable. Remove plants once their initial flush of bearing is over.

Inter-planting

Inter-planting can be defined as planting different crops in adjoining areas to take advantage of differences in growing habits, light requirements or nutrient needs. A traditional example of this technique is growing beans and corn together. Making plants share space means the individual plants may yield less, but the total garden yield will be greater because the space is being used more efficiently.

The number of ways different vegetables can be combined is limited only by your creativity. Remember, it's YOUR garden.

For successful inter-planting combinations, plan your garden around the largest, longest-growing vegetable staples like tomatoes or winter squash. Once you've decided their location, plant smaller, fast-growing vegetables around them.

In your design, consider the different growing habits of vegetable plants: for example, combine upright plants like caged tomatoes with a scattering of scallions, or grow melons around sweet corn. Inter-plant lettuce with pole beans; the lettuce will be slower to bolt when growing in the partial shade provided by the taller beans.

An inter-planted garden does not resemble a traditional garden with all the vegetables planted in smart little rows. Rather, inter-planted gardens have a mosaic effect with paths oriented around the inter-planted areas. Plants can be arranged to take advantage of contrasts in texture and color, making a garden more visually interesting. It is truly a wonder to behold.

A common error in inter-planting is crowding vegetable plants. Crowded plants yield poorly and are more subject to diseases. Consider the eventual harvest size of the vegetables you inter-plant, and space them so that at maturity they will just be touching each other. Make the inter-planted area no wider than what you can easily reach across to keep from trampling plants.

You also can avoid crowding by inter-planting fast growing vegetables with slow growing vegetables, for example, radishes or lettuce with tomatoes. By the time the tomato plants are bearing, the lettuce or radishes will be harvested. Or some of the lettuce can be removed in May to make room to sow seed of winter squash. Eventually the winter squash plants will cover the entire lettuce bed.

Similarly, vining squash or melons can be sown between trellised pea plants. The pea plants will be finished bearing about the time the melon or squash needs the trellis.

A method of inter-planting which has received notice recently is known as "square foot gardening." This technique (based on a book of the same name by Mel Bartholomew) involves planting vegetables very intensively. The growing area is divided into square foot sections. In each section, plants or seeds are carefully spaced.

For example, in one square foot you can grow 16 radishes, nine beets or one cabbage plant. This technique may be useful for container growing or where space is extremely limited, but will demand correspondingly more attention by the gardener.

Follow the usual fertilization guidelines for each crop in the inter-planting. Amend soil with compost or organic matter before planting, use a starter fertilizer or compost tea for early spring plantings, and top dress vegetables at the proper stage of their growth.

The closer spacing of inter-planted vegetables will discourage some weeds. But the weeds that do grow must still be controlled. Use small tools like onion hoes, or pull weeds by hand. Better yet, use mulches (mulch, MULCH!!) to control weeds; this will GREATLY reduce watering needs.

All gardeners can grow vegetables more efficiently by using some of the intensive growing techniques described here. Careful management is the key to successful intensive vegetable gardens. The benefits can include greater yields per square foot, and more attractive vegetable plantings.

The Pros and Cons of Intensive Gardening

Intensive Gardening is All the Rage

Intensive gardening is now fully mainstream.

Sure, you may still see the occasional backyard single row garden… but they're nowhere near as ubiquitous as they used to be.

Most home gardening is now intensive gardening, whether the gardener knows it or not.

The Rise of the Raised Bed

Square foot gardening, container gardening, biointensive gardening — all are methods of packing as much production into as small a space as possible.

What's the first thing most new gardeners do when they decide to create their very first plot of veggies in the back 40?

Build a raised bed!

Today I'm going to take a look at the pros and cons of intensive gardening. It may be the dominant method right now… but there are likely as many reasons to skip it as there are to embrace it.

The Pros of Intensive Gardening

More food—less space. That's hard to argue with!

With a well-planned intensive garden, you can maximize your yields with minimum materials. Unlike a single row garden that takes up lots of space, you can plant vegetables tightly in a little square foot garden bed or a horse trough converted into a raised bed.

You can also pack high fertility into a small space by stacking up lots of nutrition rather than trying to spread compost over a large area like you would with a traditional garden.

When you have a small backyard, why would you bother with a great big row garden when you can grow your peppers, sweet corn and bush beans in a lot less space?

Intensive gardening with bush beans

The Authorities on Intensive Gardening

I've used varying combinations of Mel Bartholomew's Square Foot Gardening and John Jeavons' methods from Grow More Vegetables in my intensive beds and have had quite good success.

There's an excellent article from Mother Earth News that takes the same tack, explaining the great results that came from the author's experimentation with combining both popular intensive gardening methods.

More Reasons to Grow Intensive

Another benefit of intensive gardening is that it's usually based on permanent beds you can protect from compaction easier than you can a big row garden which requires walking between the rows in order to weed, maintain and harvest.

Intensive gardening lets you grow a lot of food in a perfect small space — what's not to love?

Like many things in life, the initial picture doesn't give you the whole story. For example, when I was a teenager I used to have a crush on this really cute redhead, and then later.

Let's just say I ended up with a better option. Now it's time to look at the cons. (Of intensive gardening, not redheads!)

The Cons of Intensive Gardening

We have this idea that raised beds are pretty much the only way to garden at this point. Yet there are notable benefits to ditching intensive gardening for wider rows and in-ground non-raised plots.

A couple of years ago I grew a good-sized plot of corn that was watered by rainfall.

If I had planted my corn at intensive garden spacing, I would have had to water a few times a week — at least! I got a nice harvest of grain corn from that widely spaced row garden because of how much room the corn roots had to search out water, even in sand.

Intensive Beds Require Intensive Water

Our first square foot garden beds five years ago needed a lot of water compared to my corn. The spacing was very tight, as recommended in Mel Bartholomew's book, so the roots ran out of moisture rapidly.

Water! Water! Water! When it got hot out, we were watering every day… and the plants were still looking thirsty.

The yields on the space were great, though, so I can't complain too much.

It's just this: if there was ever a sustained period where the city water shut off or your well quit working, you'd lose all your harvest for that year. In a widely spaced garden, you'd likely still get some yields just because of the rainfall.

There's a reason the pioneers didn't use tight little raised beds for their crops!

Intensive Gardening Uses Permanent Beds

Another "con" of intensive gardening is the method's use of permanent beds.

I don't know about you, but I change my gardening arrangements all the time. I've had one area go from a huge patch of wildly seeded anarchy with straw paths to tight little wooden beds to cinder block beds, to rows of double-dug beds and a few perennial beds to its current mixed configuration with row of dwarf apple trees along one edge… all within five years.

If you build perfect little beds and fill them with perfect soil, you've made a commitment.

You've married the redhead!

The Bottom Line on Intensive Gardening

When everyone is doing something, it might be a good time to ask "why?" Intensive gardening has its appeal but isn't a perfect method. My bet is that its evolution is directly linked to our current level of civilization and high energy usage. If there's a breakdown in our complex world; wide, single-row gardening is likely to come back with a vengeance as we turn to the heavens for our rainfall, rather than a faucet.

Grown with rainfall, not soaker hoses!

It really is fun to try both methods in the same year as I've done. If you've got a wide open patch of lawn, why not put in some widely spaced rows of beans or corn and care for the plot with a wheel hoe? It's like going back in time… and the yields may surprise you.

Give it a go with multiple methods and see if you observe the same pros and cons of intensive gardening that I have.